Inventions And Discoveries

STERLING

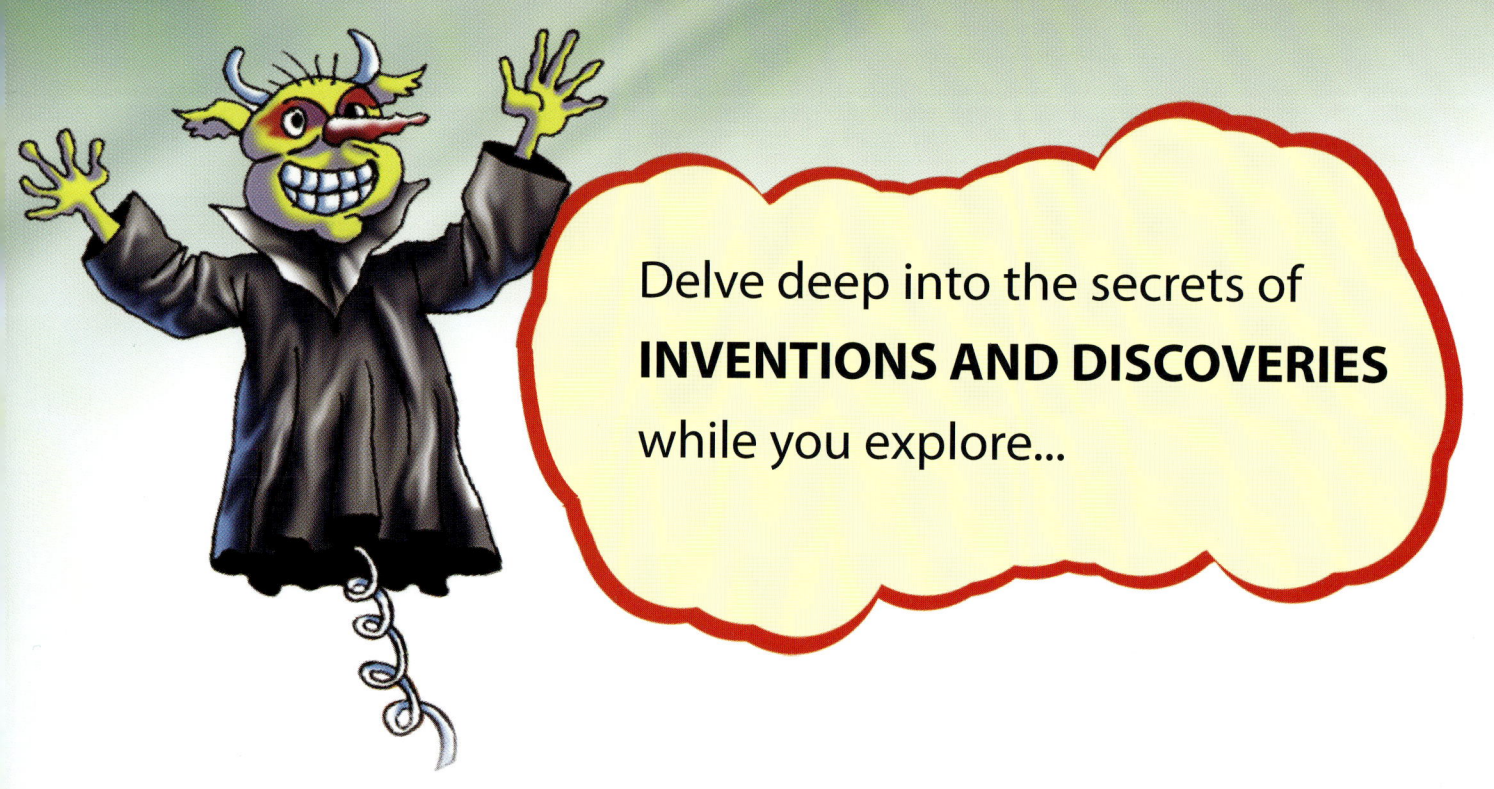

Delve deep into the secrets of **INVENTIONS AND DISCOVERIES** while you explore...

A Stroke of Luck

Making Life Easy

Inventions named after People

Inventors killed by their own Inventions

Greatest Discoveries of all time

Wonder Drugs

Light Bulb Moments

Famous Explorers

A STROKE OF LUCK

> "Louis Pasteur once said that chances favour the prepared minds."

Popsicle

- Frank Epperson was only an eleven-year-old when he invented the Popsicle and the invention was purely accidental.
He discovered it while he had left his fruit flavored soda outside on the porch with a stirring stick in it.
He left the mixture on the back porch overnight and the next day Frank found that the drink froze to the stick.

- This was the accidental invention of the first Popsicle and after almost 18 years, he started selling it with a patented name to it.

Microwave

- The invention of the microwave is considered to be one of the greatest inventions of all time.
- Dr. Percy Spencer was working as an engineer with the Raytheon Corporation. While he was testing a new vacuum tube called a magnetron, he found that the candy bar in his pocket had melted.
- Out of curiosity, Dr. Spencer decided to test it once again. He placed some corn kernels near the tube and he saw that the corn popped all over his lab.
- The Raytheon Corporation developed the first commercial microwave oven in 1947.

Ice Cream Cone

- The ice cream cone was also an accidental discovery that came into existence in 1904.
- Ernest Hamwi created the first ice cream cone for serving ice cream 1904 at the St. Louis World's Fair.
- His waffle booth was next to an ice cream vendor who ran short of dishes. Hamwi rolled a waffle and scooped icecream into it and the cone was born.
- These rolling cones came to be served with ice cream popping on top.

Champagne

- Champagne today is considered to be an integral part of every celebration.
- The monk Dom Perignon is credited with having invented Champagne, in France around 1670.
- He had in fact spent two years trying to make bubbly wine while the poor winemaker brought in one of the most original as well as unique tasting drink.
- The champagne was born out of loaded bubbles with carbon dioxide that came to gain popularity soon enough.
- Much of the world's celebrations would have remained incomplete without the accidental discovery of the champagne.

Did you know?

The sparkling bubbles in the champagne were considered to be some kind of impurity or fault initially.

Post-it Notes

- Spencer Silver worked as a senior chemist in the Central Research Lab of 3M.
- He was trying to improve the adhesive that 3M used for tape, when he discovered less sticky glue.
- The glue he created could hold paper together, but wasn't strong enough to maintain the bond when pulled on.
- Post-it notes came into existence with the accidental work when on one Sunday, four years later, another 3M scientist named Arthur Fry was singing in the church's choir.
- He used markers to keep his place in the hymnal, but they kept falling out of the book. Fry used Silver's adhesive to coat his markers.
- These sticky mark notes became very famous and later 3M began distributing Post-it Notes nationwide in 1980.

Potato Chips

- George Crum, a Native American, was employed as a chef at an elegant resort in Saratoga Springs, New York.
- One dinner guest found French fries too thick and rejected the order.
- Crum decided to produce the French fries too thin and crisp to skewer with a fork which began to appear on the menu as Saratoga Chips, a house specialty.
- This is how he came up with the idea of chips which became a instant hit and featured on the menus of several restaurants.

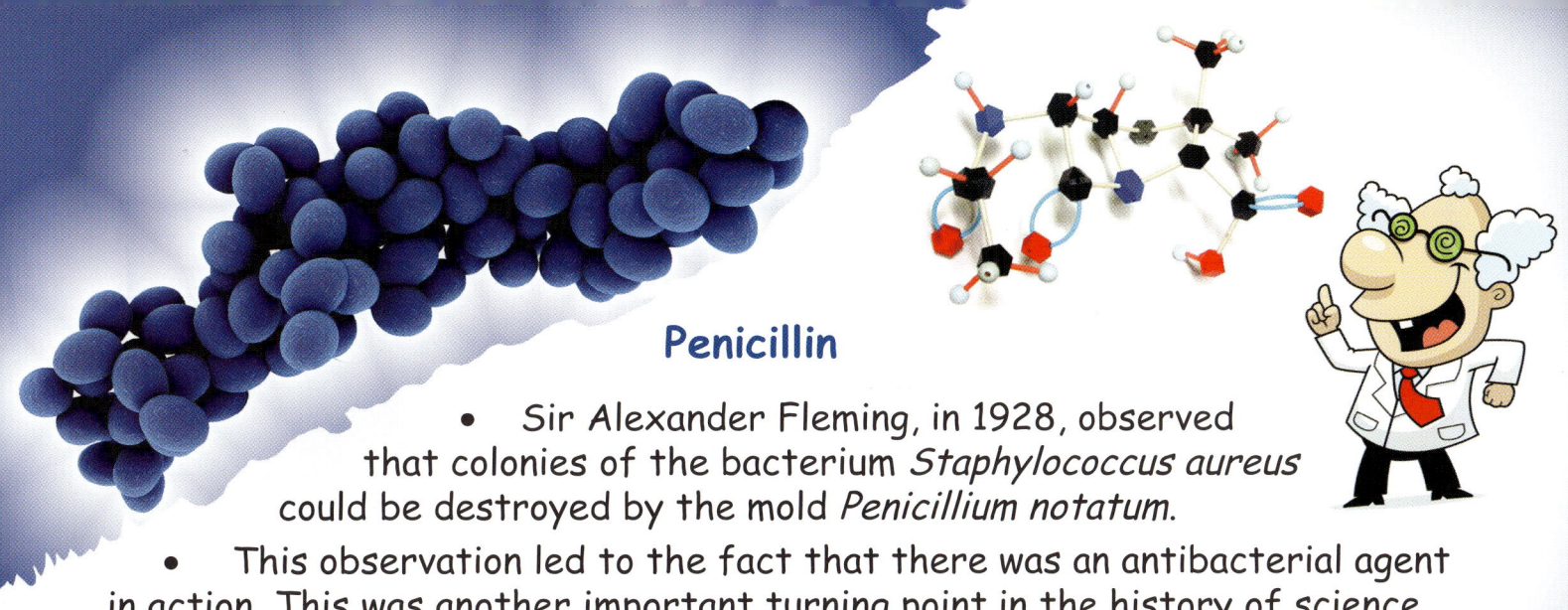

Penicillin

- Sir Alexander Fleming, in 1928, observed that colonies of the bacterium *Staphylococcus aureus* could be destroyed by the mold *Penicillium notatum*.
- This observation led to the fact that there was an antibacterial agent in action. This was another important turning point in the history of science.
- He observed that a plate culture of Staphylococcus had been contaminated by a blue-green mold and that colonies of bacteria adjacent to the mold were being destroyed.
- Alexander Fleming grew the mold in a pure culture and found that it produced a substance that killed a number of disease-causing bacteria.
- He named the substance as penicillin, after *Penicillium notatum*.

The Pacemaker

- The invention of pacemaker has been one of the breakthrough inventions in medical history.
- Hopps was trained as an electrical engineer. In 1941, he joined the National Research Council where he conducted research on hypothermia.
- While he was experimenting with radio frequency heating to restore body temperature, he concluded that if the heart stopped beating due to cooling, it could be started again by artificial stimulation using mechanical or electric means. Thus the world's first cardiac pacemaker was invented in 1950.
- His device was far too large to be implanted inside of the human body. It was an external pacemaker.

MAKING LIFE EASY

These are the most important inventions that the world has ever received. They have definitely changed the shape and structure of the world in many different ways. Without these the world would not have had half the fun it has now.

Telephone

- A practical telephone was invented independently by two men working in the United States, Elisha Gray and Scottish-born Alexander Graham Bell.
- Both men filed for a patent on their designs at the New York patent office on February 14, 1876, but Bell beat Gray by only two hours.
- Bell initially wanted to invent a modified telegraph that could send multiple messages or signals at the same time.
- During experimentation, the concept of making a device that could transmit speech through electricity, struck Bell's mind.
- In 1875, Bell along with his assistant and electrician, Thomas A. Watson, continued experimenting to build an apparatus that could transmit sound.
- Finally, on 10th March, 1876, Bell spoke the first words through a telephone, "Mr. Watson, come here, I want to see you", and they were clearly heard on the other side.

Prof. Bell's vibrating reed-used for a receiver

Alexander Graham Bell's first telephone

Ball-point Pen

- Laszlo Biro was a Hungarian journalist who invented the first ballpoint pen in 1938.
- He noticed that the ink used in newspaper printing press dried quickly and left the paper dry and smudge-free.
- This gave him the idea to use the same type of ink for writing instruments.
- But the ink used for printing was much thicker as compared to normal ink and ink would not flow from a regular pen nib.
- To overcome this problem, he fitted his pen with a tiny ball bearing in its tip.
- Moving along the paper, the ball rotates picking up ink from the ink cartridge and leaving it on the paper.

LIGHT BULB MOMENTS

Aeroplane

Wilbur Wright and Orville Wright invented the airplane, which they patented as a "flying machine".
The first engine-powered airplane to fly was the Kitty Hawk on December 17, 1903.

X-Ray

Like most other discoveries, this too was accidental. A German physicist, Wilhelm Conrad Röntgen is credited for the discovery of x-rays.
Wilhelm Röntgen was conducting experiments in his laboratory on the effects of cathode rays when he discovered X-rays in 1895.
Röntgen described a new form of radiation that allowed him to photograph objects that were hidden behind opaque shield.

Bone China

Bone china is a type of porcelain that is made with animal bone.
Before the invention of bone china, most porcelain was either hard or soft and came from China.
England is the birthplace of bone china. It was created around 1800 by Josiah Spode I, a famous potter and owner of the Spode porcelain factory.
It combines bone ash (animal bone) with the hard-paste porcelain ingredients kaolin and china stone. It is fired at 1200 – 1300 °C.

Aspirin

- The leaves and bark of some trees like the willow contain a substance called salicin, which relieves the pain to some extent.
- People in the olden days used to chew the leaves or bark of such trees in order to get relief from pain. In 1853 a French chemist, Charles Frederick von Gerhardt while experimenting with salicin in the laboratory came up with acetylsalicylic acid which is today known as aspirin.

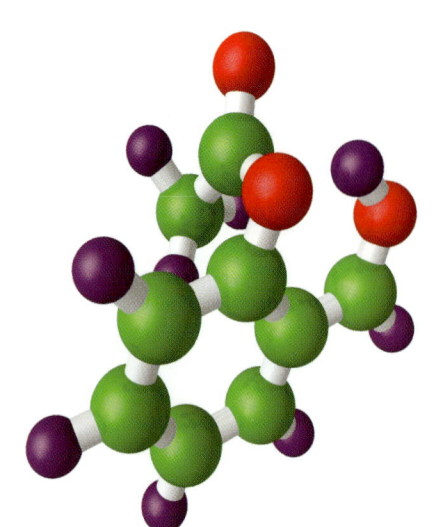

- Gerhardt tested the substance on a few people and came to the conclusion that chewing bark was better and subsequently he lost all interest in it.
- In the 1890s a German chemist, Felix Hofmann prepared a batch of salicin and tested it on his father.
- He discovered that his father felt the pain receding.
- Soon aspirin began to be marketed in tablet form. Today it is considered a wonder drug used as a cure for multiple diseases.

WONDER DRUGS

Cure for Malaria

- Malaria parasites are believed to have originated in Africa. Many fossils of mosquitoes up to 30 million years old have been found.
- Hippocrates, who is regarded as the "Father of Medicine", was the first to describe the manifestations of the disease, and relate them to the time of year and to where the patients lived.
- In 1879, Alphonse Laveran began researching to explain the role of the particles of a black pigment found in the blood of people suffering from malaria and found the presence of certain parasites.
- Laveran published his first great work on these parasites in 1884.
- **Ronald Ross** was an English physician who studied malaria in India as a member of the Indian Medical Service during 1881-99.
- He undertook the experimental testing of the mosquito-theory, proposed by Laveran.
- While investigating the claim of his contemporaries that malaria was transmitted through mosquito bites, Dr. Ross discovered his true vocation to seek a cure.

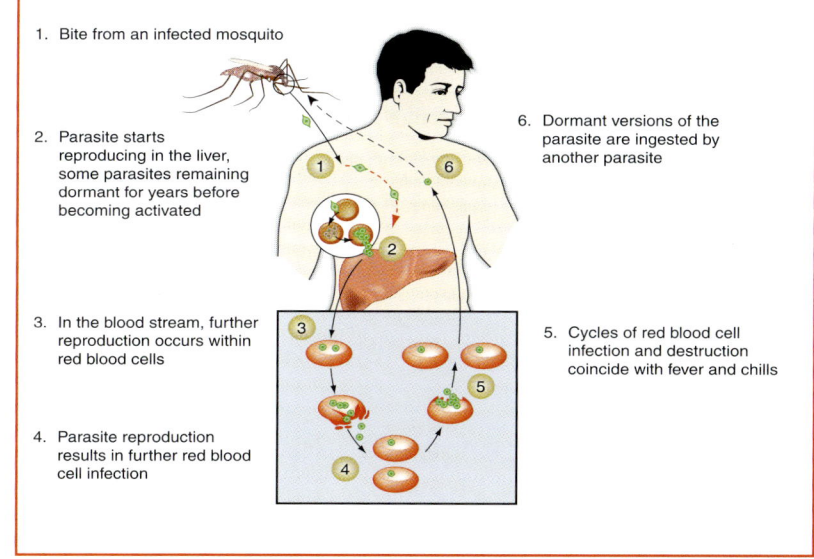

Amazing!

The cinchona tree, also known as quina quina, gives the drug quinine, which has been used for the cure of malaria ever since.

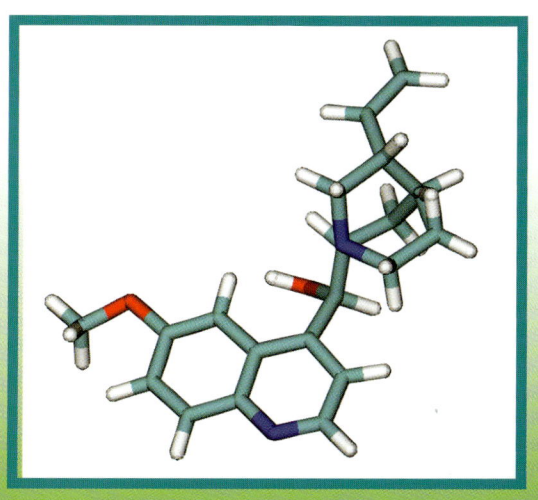

Hot Air Balloons

- The birth of air balloon flight came in the year 1782, with a discovery of two brothers Joseph and Etienne Montgolfier.
- They discovered that the hot air is lighter than cold air and this led to the invention of a small silk balloon.
- These balloons were also used for observation in World War I.
- The balloon was inflated with the heat from burning straw, wool and dried horse manure underneath the balloon.
- The heater warmed the air inside the balloon, making it lighter than the surrounding atmosphere, and caused the balloon and its cargo to rise.
- The first passengers to fly in the balloon were a sheep, a duck and a rooster.
- On the 21st of November, 1783, a hot air balloon was launched in Paris which rose 500 feet and finally landing in the vineyards nearby.
- One of the persons on this balloon was Pilatre de Rozier, from whose name the word "pilot" is derived.

Gravity

- There are four fundamental interactions: gravity, electromagnetism, strong nuclear force and weak nuclear force.
- Sir Issac Newton discovered gravity nearly three centuries ago.
- He was a mathematician and a physicist.
- Many people have the image that he was sitting under an apple tree when an apple fell and hit him on the head, thus giving him the idea for gravity.
- He discovered that there existed a force that is required to change the speed or direction of a moving object.
- Understanding gravity helped a lot in understanding how the Earth and planets move.

DNA: Deoxyribonucleic Acid

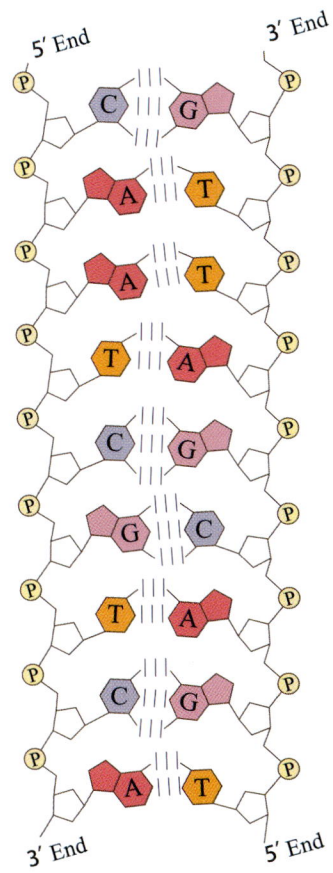

- DNA was first identified in the late 1860s by Swiss chemist Friedrich Miescher.
- The discovery of DNA shaped our understanding of genetics, leading to applications in the field of forensics, genetic engineering and so on.
- On April 1953, James Watson and Francis Crick presented the structure of the DNA-helix, the molecule that carries genetic information from one generation to the other.
- They proposed that the DNA molecule exists in the form of a three-dimensional double helix.

Micro-organisms

- Antony van Leeuwenhoek, a Dutch cloth merchant, was the first person to see bacteria.
- During the 1660s he started to grind glass lenses to make better magnifying lenses so he could examine the weave of cloth more easily.
- He excelled at lens grinding and achieved magnifications up to 500 times life-size.
- He used his best lens to look at a sample of pond water, and saw that it was teeming with tiny living things.
- It was he who discovered bacteria, free-living and parasitic microscopic protists, sperm cells, blood cells, microscopic nematodes and rotifers, and much more.

- A greek philosopher and astronomer, Aristarchus of Samos (310BC-230BC) first presented the theory that the Sun was at the centre of the solar system (heliocentrism) but his ideas were rejected in favour of the theories of Ptolemy and Aristotle that the Earth was at the centre (geocentrism).

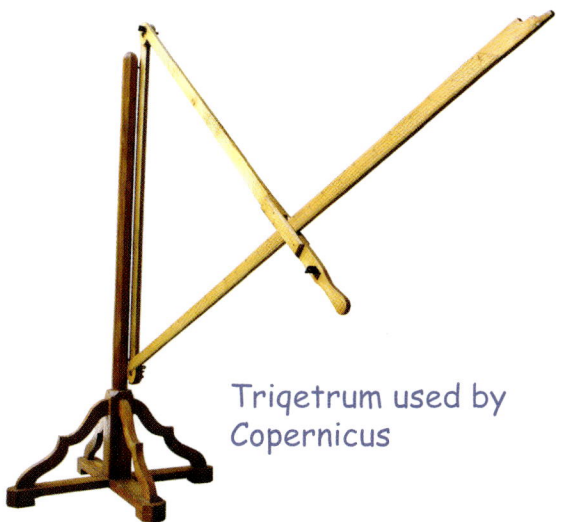

Triqetrum used by Copernicus

- Copernicus researched, supported and published the heliocentric theory in the 16th Century.
- His theory is considered to be one of the most important discoveries ever, and is the fundamental starting point of modern astronomy.
- Copernicus held that the Earth is another planet revolving around the fixed sun once a year, and turning on its axis once a day.

GREATEST DISCOVERIES OF ALL TIME

There have been many great discoveries throughout the history of humanity, so that it is difficult to objectively determine which discoveries should be considered the greatest.

To be great, a discovery needs to reveal to us concepts that hadn't been considered or fully understood before. Also, a great discovery is one that propels humanity forward, advancing our understanding of the Universe. It is also worth noting that many discoveries would not have been possible if it weren't for earlier discoveries that laid the building blocks. That being said, there are several discoveries that warrant recognition as some of the greatest discoveries of all time.

The Sun is the Center of the Solar System

- The solar system is made up of the Sun and the objects that orbit around it. These include EIGHT planets, and their satellites.

- Several astronomers can be credited with this discovery but Nicolaus Copernicus was the first astronomer to suggest that the Earth was not the center of the solar system.

Alexander Bogdanov

- Alexander Bogdanov was a Russian physician, economist, philosopher, natural scientist, writer and polymath who wrote science fiction books.
- He believed that blood transfusions could extend life and rejuvenate health.
- He was the founder of the world's first institution devoted entirely to the field of blood transfusion.
- In 1924, Bogdanov started his blood transfusion experiments, apparently hoping to achieve eternal youth or at least partial rejuvenation.
- He pioneered the blood transfusion. He gave himself 11 blood transfusions and was very satisfied.
- But the twelfth transfusion cost him his life, when he took the blood of a student suffering from malaria and tuberculosis.

William Bullock

- William Bullock was born in Greenville, New York in 1813.
- He invented the web rotary printing press.
- William Bullock's invention, in 1863, represents the beginning of the modern, web-fed newspaper press, which works from curved, stereotype plates and prints on both sides of the paper in one pass through the machine.
- Several years after its invention, his foot was crushed while installing a new machine in Philadelphia.
- On April 3, 1867, Bullock tried to kick a driving belt onto a pulley while making some adjustments in his new press and he crushed his leg. After a few days, he developed gangrene and died on 12th April, 1867.

INVENTORS KILLED BY THEIR OWN INVENTIONS

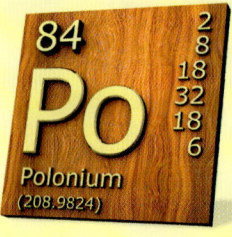 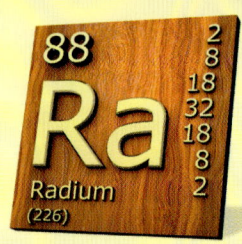

Marie Curie (1867–1934)

- Marie Curie was a pioneer in the field of radioactivity, the first person honored with two Nobel Prizes, and the first female professor at the University of Paris.
- She invented the process to isolate radium after co-discovering the radioactive elements, radium and polonium.
- Under her personal direction, the world's first studies were conducted into the treatment of neoplasms ("cancers"), using radioactive isotopes.
- She died of aplastic anemia as a result of prolonged exposure to ionizing radiation.

Franz Reichelt (1879–1912)

- Franz Reichelt was an Austrian tailor who designed an overcoat that would act as a parachute.
- Reichelt was known by the locals as the flying tailor.
- He used his skills as a tailor to create an overcoat that he was sure would allow him to fly, glide or float to the ground without harm.
- He demonstrated his invention with his only jump of 60 meters from the first deck of the Eiffel Tower.
- This turned out to be a disaster and he died.

Diesel Engine - Rudolf Diesel

- Rudolf Diesel was born in Paris on March 18, 1858.
- While an employee of the Linde firm, Diesel became fascinated with the theoretical work of the French physicist Nicholas Carnot, which presented the principles of the modern internal combustion engine.
- Rudolf Diesel designed many heat engines, including a solar-powered air engine.
- In 1893, he published a paper describing an engine with combustion within a cylinder, the internal combustion engine.
- In 1894, he filed for a patent for his new invention, named as diesel engine.
- His engine was the first to prove that fuel could be ignited without a spark.
- He operated his first successful engine in 1897.

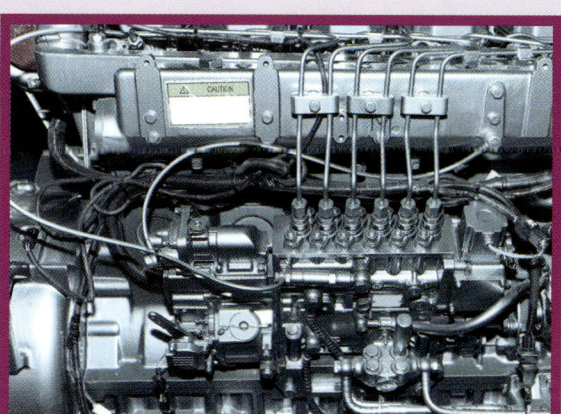

Nikola Tesla

- Nikola Tesla was born in Smiljan, Croatia on July 9, 1856.
- He worked as an electrical engineer in Budapest and later immigrated to the United States in 1884 to work at the Edison Machine Works.
- He invented the induction motor and the transformer known as the Tesla coil.
- He also discovered the rotating magnetic field principle.
- There are many inventions to his credit like fluorescent lighting, the Tesla induction motor and the Tesla coil.

INVENTIONS NAMED AFTER PEOPLE

Sandwich – Earl of Sandwich

The term "sandwich" originated in 1762 in London, while slices of bread with meat and cheese had been eaten since the dawn of the loaf of bread.

One night during very late hours, an English nobleman, John Montagu, was busy gambling. He did not stop for a meal despite being hungry.

The legend goes that John Montagu called for such a dish to be served to him, so he could remain at the gaming table without breaking for supper.

The Earl wanted to continue his gambling while eating his snack.

This incident gave us the quick-food product that we now know as the sandwich.

Saxophone – Adolphe Sax

- Saxophone was invented by Antoine Joseph Adolphe Sax, a Belgian musical instrument designer.
- Adolphe's first important invention was an improvement of the bass clarinet design which he patented at the age of twenty-four.

- In 1840, Sax invented the clarinette-bourdon, an early design of contrabass clarinet. He developed the saxophone instrument during this period and patented it in 1846.
- The saxophone was invented for use in both orchestras and concert bands.

Telescope

A telescope is a device that lets us view distant objects.

The first refracting telescope was invented by Hans Lippershey in 1608.

Lippershey was a German-born Dutch lens maker who demonstrated the first refracting telescope in 1608, made from two lenses.

He applied for a patent for this optical refracting telescope (using 2 lenses) in 1608.

In 1609, a man named Galileo Galilei from Italy used this discovery to build the first telescope.

He was the first person to use a telescope to observe and look into space.

He discovered the rings of Saturn in 1610, and was the first person to see the four major moons of Jupiter.

Atomic Bomb

- J. Robert Oppenheimer was born in New York City.
- Oppenheimer was the son of German immigrants and textile importers.

When World War II began, Oppenheimer eagerly became involved in the efforts to develop an atomic bomb, which were already taking up much of the time and facilities of Lawrence's Radiation Laboratory at Berkeley.

He was invited to take over work on neutron calculations, and in June 1942 General Leslie Groves appointed Oppenheimer as the scientific director of the Manhattan Project.

The joint work of the scientists at Los Alamos resulted in the first nuclear explosion at Alamagordo on July 16, 1945, which Oppenheimer named "Trinity."

Fire Extinguisher

- George William Manby was born on November 28, 1765 in Denver, Norfolk.
- He was an English author and inventor as well.
- He designed the first modern form of fire extinguisher.
- Manby invented the first portable pressurized fire extinguisher in 1813 and named it the "Extincteur".
- This consisted of a copper vessel of 3 gallons of potassium carbonate solution contained within compressed air.

Gas Mask and Traffic Signal

- Garrett Augustus Morgan was born in 1877 in Paris, Kentucky.
- He was an African-American inventor and a businessman.
- He was the first person to patent a traffic signal.
- He also developed the gas mask.
- Morgan patented a traffic signal on November 20, 1923. This was the first traffic signal patented, but not the first invented.

First Artificial Refrigerator

- First artificial refrigerator was developed by the Scottish chemist William Cullen.
- He carried out his research in Glasglow University in 1748.

Postage Stamp

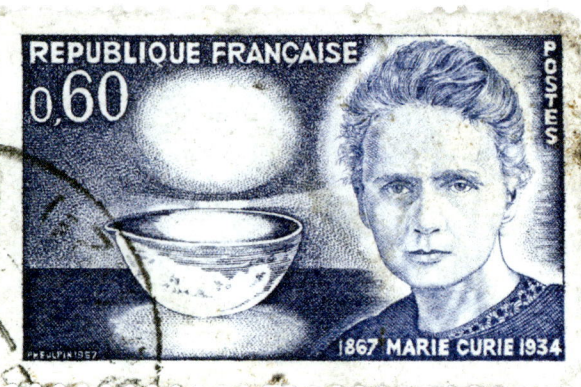

- Rowland Hill was born in 1795 in Kidderminster, near Birmingham.
- Rowland Hill invented the prepaid postage stamp.
- He was an important Victorian reformer who wanted to improve living conditions for everyone. This included making the postage cheaper and affordable for all the people.
- During those times people had to pay a certain amount depending on how many sheets of paper they used and how far the letter travelled.
- This was very expensive. He believed that if more people were able to send letters, then more people would learn to read and write which would greatly improve their lives.

Did you know?

In 1837, Hill wrote an important booklet called 'Post Office Reform'

Textile

The term 'Textile' originated from a Latin word 'texere' which means 'to weave.'
The history of textile is almost as old as that of human civilization.
The oldest recorded indication of using fiber comes with the invention of flax and wool fabric at the excavation of Swiss lake inhabitants during the 6th and 7th century BC.
In India the culture of silk was introduced in 400AD, while spinning of cotton traces back to 3000BC.
The world's first textile mill was found by Francis Cabot Lowell.

Printing Press

Johannes Gutenberg was a German craftsman and printer who invented the first printing press that was movable in 1450.
His new press could print a page every three minutes.

Sports Shoes

Adolph (Adi) Dassler invented spiked shoes for track and field.
Four years later Adi and his brother Rudolph (Rudi) founded the German sports shoe company Gebrüder Dassler Schuhfabrik.
Following the split between two brothers, Adi renamed the company as Adidas.
Registered in 1949, Adidas is currently based in Herzogenaurach, Germany.

FAMOUS EXPLORERS

Ferdinand Magellan: Ferdinand Magellan was a Portuguese explorer and is credited for circumnavigating the Earth for the first time.

Amerigo Vespucci: He was the Italian explorer and navigator, and also one of the early explorers of the New World. It is generally believed that America got its name from his Latin name Americus Vespucci.

Hernan Cortes: He was a Spanish conquistador and explorer. He is best known for conquering the Mexico and the Aztec Empire.

James Cook: He was a great explorer because he was the first to lead a sailing expedition around the world successfully. He commanded the Endeavor on his first trip to the Pacific, an expedition to observe Venus for the Royal Society. He landed at Tahiti and became the first European to discover and chart the coasts of New Zealand, Australia, and New Guinea. On another three-year voyage, Cook explored the ice fields of Antarctica.

Vasco da Gama: He was a Portuguese explorer and is very famous for an expedition at the end of the 15th century that opened the sea route to India by way of the Cape of Good Hope at the southern tip of Africa.

Francis Drake: Sir Francis Drake was a British explorer and slave-trader. Francis Drake achieved lasting fame as a result of his association with the victory against the Spanish Armada. He was a loyal subject of Elizabeth I. From 1577 to 1580, Drake circumnavigated the world.

William Dampier: William was an explorer and sea captain, and is one of the most highly regarded map-makers and navigators of all time. Dampier led several voyages of mapping and exploration around the world. He was the first Englishman to explore or map parts of New Holland, Australia and New Guinea. He was also the first person to circumnavigate the world thrice.

Discovery of America

- The American continent was discovered by Christopher Columbus
- His objective was to sail to Asia (the Indies) where the riches of gold, pearls and spice were present in abundance.
- In 1484 the Portuguese were already working on a way to Asia and rejected Christopher's theories.
- Columbus moved to Spain for permission but faced rejections from the Spanish royal commission as well.
- His hard work finally paid off on April 1492 when Ferdinand V, king of Castile, and Queen Isabella agreed to sponsor his expedition.
- Columbus led his three ships, namely the Nina, the Pinta and the Santa Maria out of the Spanish port on August 3, 1492.
- He first sailed to the Canary Islands, where he stayed for a month, and then he started the five week voyage across the ocean.
- He faked the logbook to make his crew believe they had covered a smaller distance than they actually had.
- There is still much discussion about which island he reached.

Did You Know?

Christopher Columbus made a total of four voyages from Spain to what he called the New World, between 1492 and 1504.

The Pinta